ORA DE DESPERTAR

TIME TO WAKE UP

This book is dedicated to Irit & Dalia,
Ladino's next generation

Illustrations & Design by Miriam Ross
www.miriamzross.com

ISBN-13: 978-1545296165
ISBN-10: 1545296162

This book is part of the
Ora de Despertar Ladino children's project
produced by Aroeste Music.

To learn more please visit www.saraharoeste.com

www.saraharoeste.com

Author's Note

Ladino, or Judeo-Spanish, is the language spoken by Sephardic Jews, those Jews whose families can be traced back to Spain in the 15th century. For hundreds of years Ladino was the primary language spoken by Jews who settled in the Mediterranean and North Africa, after being expelled from Spain in 1492. As Jews dispersed, their Spanish became combined with bits of Hebrew, Portuguese, Italian, French, Turkish and more. Although the Ladino language is fading today, it is still spoken by and binds together Sephardic Jews scattered across the globe.

The Modeh Ani prayer is a simple prayer recited immediately upon waking up in the morning. The Book of Lamentations states that "The Lord's mercies are not consumed, surely His compassions do not fail. They are new every morning; great is Your faithfulness." (Lam. 3:22-23) The great Jewish legal code, the Shulchan Aruch, interpreted these lines to mean that each morning, God renews every person as a new creation. Every morning when we wake up, we have a brand-new soul for another day. For this, we are grateful! Thankfulness is a central theme in Judaism. The fact that the Modeh Ani prayer is the very first thing we are supposed to think about in the morning, sets the tone for our entire day. Our first waking moments are to say thank you for letting us wake up!

Ora de Despertar is the Ladino way of saying Time to Wake Up! By using Ladino words to demonstrate the rituals of waking up, and connecting it to the Modeh Ani prayer (or in Ladino, Atorgo yo), the reader can see how universal are the themes of thanks and mornings – no matter the language. Jews from all over the world can be grateful for the chance to approach each day anew.

I thank you, living and everlasting Source of life,
for You have graciously returned my soul within me. Great is your faithfulness.

Atorgo yo delantre de ti rey bivo i ferme ke izites tornar en mi mi alma.
Por piadad grande de tu fieldad

מוֹדָה אֲנִי הָאשה אומרת: מוֹדָה לְפָנֶיךָ

מֶלֶךְ חַי וְקַיָּם שֶׁהֶחֱזַרְתָּ בִּי נִשְׁמָתִי בְּחֶמְלָה, רַבָּה אֱמוּנָתֶךָ:

Modeh ani l'fanecha, Melech chai v'kayam,
She-hechezarta bi nishmati b'chemlah, Rabbah emunatecha.

El sol briya en mi ventana

Las solombras baylan

Los pasharos djugan afuera

I sus kantes kantan

The sun shines through my window
The shadows dance along
The birds all play outside
As they sing their song

ORA DE DESPERTAR!

TIME TO WAKE UP!

Ora de despertar, ora de despertar
Ora de aferrar el día!
Ora de despertar, ora de despertar
Es un nuevo día!

Time to wake up, time to wake up
Time to catch the day!
Time to wake up, time to wake up
It's a brand new day!

First I stretch my arms
And then I do my toes

Estiro los brasos

I los dedos de los piezes

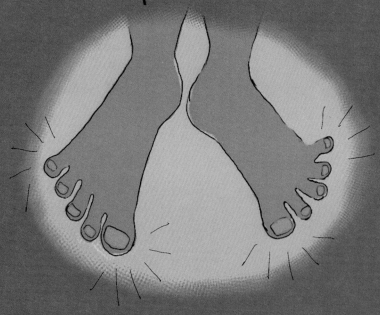

Traigo las piernas

Asta las orejas

Then I lift my legs
Up until my earlobes

modeh ani atorgoryo thank you

Ora de despertar, ora de despertar
Ora de aferrar el dia!
Ora de despertar, ora de despertar
Es un muevo dia!

Time to wake up, time to wake up
Time to catch the day!
Time to wake up, time to wake up
It's a brand new day!

I jump out of my bed
I dress myself in clothes

Salto de la kama

Me meto mis panyos

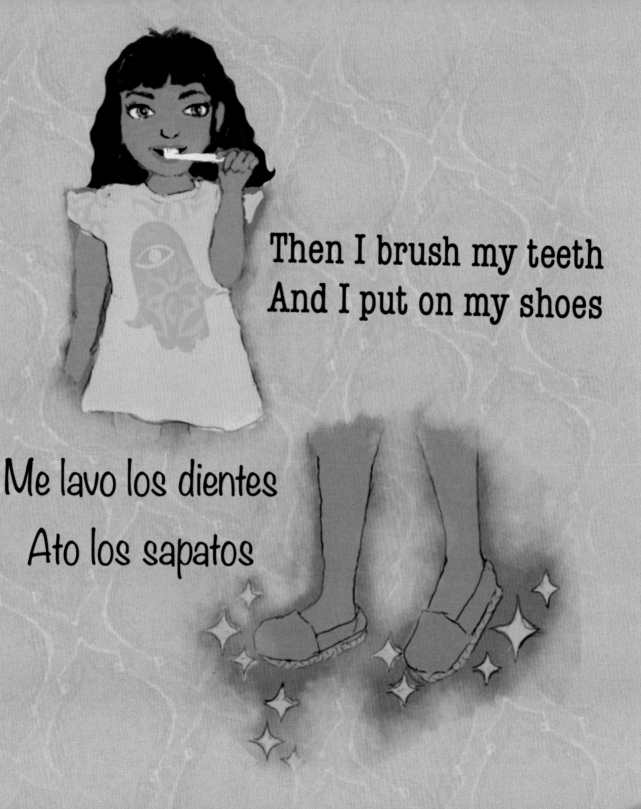

Then I brush my teeth
And I put on my shoes

Me lavo los dientes
Ato los sapatos

Ora de despertar, ora de despertar
Ora de aferrar el dia!
Ora de despertar, ora de despertar
Es un muevo dia!

Time to wake up, time to wake up
Time to catch the day!
Time to wake up, time to wake up
It's a brand new day!

Saludo a mis ermanos,
Mi perro i mis gatos

modeh ani atorgo yo ithank you

I greet my siblings hello,
My dog and my kittens

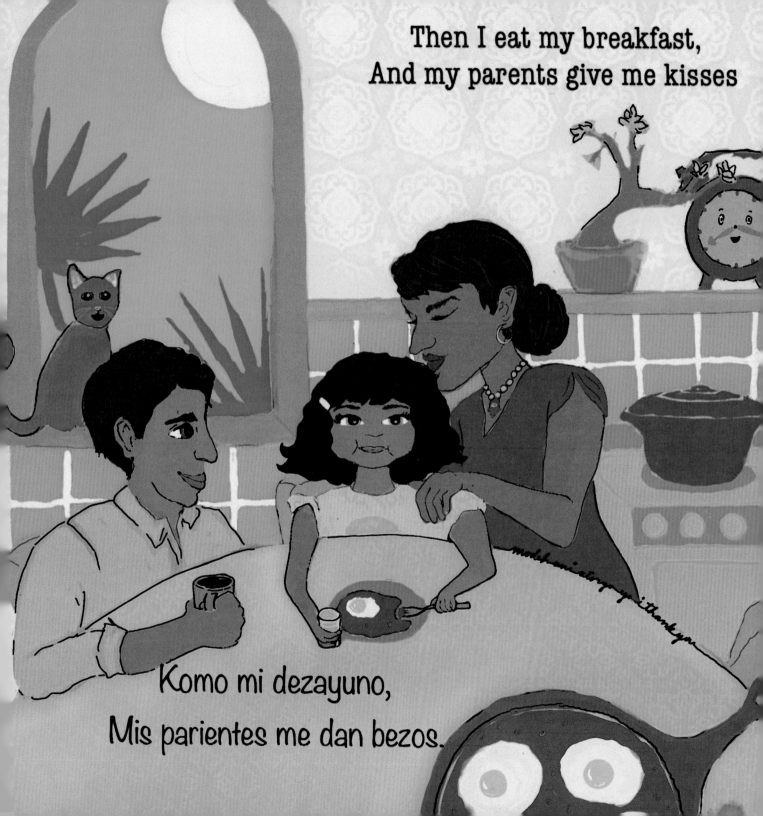

Then I eat my breakfast,
And my parents give me kisses

Komo mi dezayuno,
Mis parientes me dan bezos.

Ora de despertar, ora de despertar
Ora de aferrar el dia!
Ora de despertar, ora de despertar
Es un muevo dia!

Time to wake up, time to wake up
Time to catch the day!
Time to wake up, time to wake up
It's a brand new day!

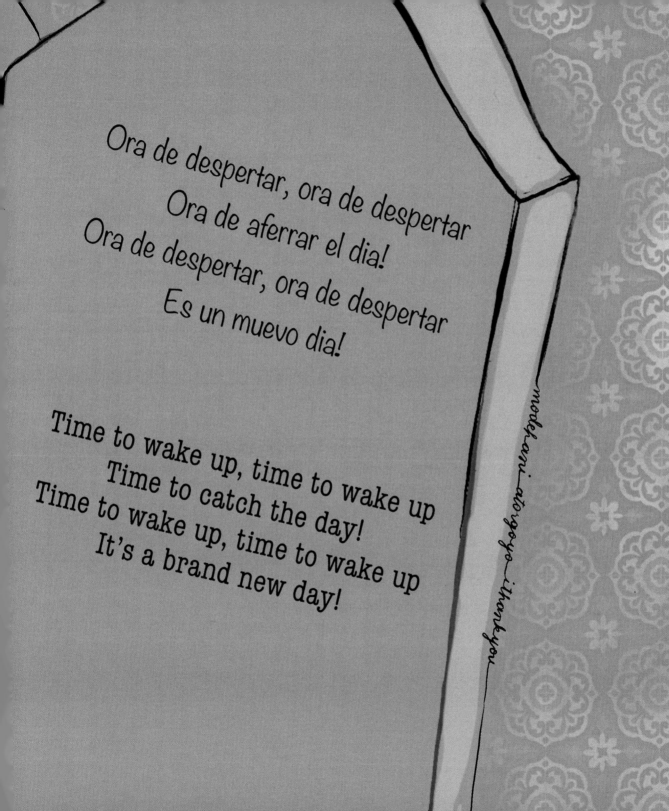

Questions for Discussion

What are some of the things you do to get ready in the morning?

What are some of the things you are thankful for when you wake up?

What are some ways that you express your thanks to people?

About the Author

With ancestral roots from Greece and Macedonia (via Medieval Spain), American-born Sarah Aroeste works to preserve Ladino culture for a new generation. A composer, singer, and children's book author, Aroeste travels the globe combining traditional Sephardic flavors with her signature contemporary style. She lives in Western Massachusetts with her husband and two daughters, her muses for revitalizing Ladino tradition.

About the Illustrator

A graphic designer and visual artist, Miriam Ross attributes much of her visual inspiration to the elaborate design and brightly saturated hues of Mediterranean and Western European culture. A graduate of Clark University and the Siena Art Institute in Siena, Italy, Ross has since spent time living in Spain and Italy, collecting colors and memories that inform her work.

Made in United States
North Haven, CT
10 April 2022